STRONGHEART

STRONGHEART

THE WORLD'S FIRST MOVIE STAR DOG

Emily Arnold McCully

HENRY HOLT AND COMPANY • NEW YORK

This is the story of Etzel von Oeringen, who became the first movie star dog. His life began a long way from Hollywood. Etzel was born in Germany during World War I. He was the son and grandson of champion police dogs.

He was bred to be alert, brave, strong, and perfectly loyal.

He learned to jump over a tall
man's head without ruffling a hair.

He could sniff out a criminal
and tackle him in a bound.

Etzel never played. He only knew how to work.

After World War I ended, Etzel was sent to America
to be sold. Etzel found himself in a kennel outside New York
City. He had been taught to guard his territory, wherever it
might be. So that is what he did.

At that time, silent movies were America's passion. A movie director named Larry Trimble, who was also an animal trainer, wanted to try something new: make a movie that would star a dog—not just as someone's pet, but as the hero of the story.

Larry and his wife, Jane, who was a screenwriter, began searching for the right dog.

One day, they visited Etzel's kennel. Impatient to see the young champion, Larry barged directly into the yard.

CRASH!

Etzel hurled himself through a window and charged at them. Jane screamed and started to run.

"HALT AND KEEP STILL!" Larry yelled at her. Jane stopped. So did Etzel.

Etzel stood at attention, searching Larry's face for his next command.

"Here," Larry said, pointing to the ground beside him.
Etzel marched to the spot, still alert, and waited to see
if Larry was friend or foe.

Larry knew this was a well-trained dog.
"He's the one!" Larry said. "He knows his duty but he
thinks for himself. And to top it all, he has real star power!"
They took Etzel home with them to Hollywood.

At Larry and Jane's house, Etzel marched inside ahead
of them. He sniffed the corners of every room, every closet,
every cupboard, like a detective. Then he signaled to Larry
and Jane that it was safe to enter.

"I hope we haven't made a mistake," said Jane.
"Etzel doesn't know how to play. Before he can act in
movies, he will have to learn to relax and have fun."

"You'll see," Larry said. "I'll teach him."

Etzel marched like a soldier. Larry taught him to walk like a dog.

To teach Etzel how to play, Larry first had to show him how to let down his guard. Larry pushed Etzel off balance. "Play!" he said every time Etzel toppled over.

After a few weeks, Etzel realized it was a game.

Then Larry decided Etzel
was ready for a playmate.
He got him a kitten.

Etzel quickly learned he had
to be careful with kittens!

"He sees that playing is fun, but there are rules,"
Larry said. "It's just like acting."

In time, Etzel
learned to play ball,
to fetch, and to chase.

He loved his toys. He would take each toy out of the closet, play for a while, and then carefully put it back where it belonged.

His favorite was a mouse. He wouldn't let anyone else touch it.

After playtime, Larry read to Etzel.

Larry and Jane also introduced Etzel to their friends.
Everyone thought he was charming.
"He's a real star!" they said.

Jane began writing the
script for the movie.

Larry and Etzel became so close that when Larry felt like relaxing, he would find Etzel lying at his feet. When he felt like taking a walk, Etzel was already waiting at the door with his leash.

"He can read my mind," Larry said.

He and Jane noticed that when they felt sad, Etzel looked downcast. When they felt happy, Etzel seemed happy too. They found that they could prompt Etzel to show any emotion the screenplay might require.

"He'll need a screen name," said Jane.

"I've got it!" Larry said. "He's strong and he has a big heart."

"STRONGHEART!" cried Jane happily.

"Let's make our movie!" said Larry.

They began filming Jane's script, *The Silent Call.*

The camera loved Strongheart. If a scene was sad, Larry made a long face and Strongheart copied him. When the heroine was in danger, Larry looked brave and determined. So did Strongheart.

Strongheart performed all his own stunts, including a daring mountaintop rescue.

When the head of the movie
studio saw Strongheart's soulful
close-ups, he wept.

Soon *The Silent Call*—the first movie to star a dog—
opened in theaters everywhere. All shows were sold out.

The studio was ecstatic. Strongheart was sent on a nationwide publicity tour. He rode in a private railroad car, attended by a press agent and a valet.

He slept in top hotels and dined in fine restaurants. Everywhere he went, huge crowds gathered. Strongheart was front page news in papers from coast to coast.

When Strongheart and Larry came home, they took a well-deserved rest.

One day, a man who said he was a journalist from New York demanded to know how Strongheart had become an actor. What were the secrets of his training?

"I'll introduce you," Larry said. "He's right outside."

As soon as Strongheart saw the strange man, he shot to attention. Larry hadn't seen him look that way since their first meeting. He was a police dog again!

Strongheart charged. He grabbed the visitor and threw him flat.

Larry quickly managed to pull Strongheart off the man.

"Your dog is finished!" cried the man. "He's a killer attack dog and should be kept in a pen!"

An hour later, the studio head called.

"Your dog has gone berserk! We're trying to keep it out of the papers. We are canceling his next picture."

Larry and Jane were heartbroken. What could have made their gentle dog behave that way? Was Strongheart's movie career really over?

Strongheart studied Larry's face. Then he went to his toy closet and returned with his mouse. He offered it to Larry.

"Thanks, old boy," Larry said. "You always know how I feel."

Two days later, Strongheart's attack was explained. The man was not a journalist at all. He was a dog trainer trying to steal Larry's secrets so that he could get his own dog into the movies.

"Strongheart knew he was lying," said Larry. "He sniffed him out! He's a hero onscreen and off."

Strongheart went on to make more hit movies. The studio
decided he should have a mate. Strongheart got to pick her:
Lady Jule. They co-starred in a movie and raised a family
together. All of their puppies became movie actors too.

Strongheart had been the first—but not the last—
great movie star dog.

AUTHOR'S NOTE

This book is based on the real life of Etzel von Oeringen, known as Strongheart, whose hugely popular movies introduced Americans to the German shepherd. The breed, developed in Germany at the end of the nineteenth century, was highly intelligent, brave, and loyal, and was adopted by the German army and police.

Strongheart was born in 1917 and came to the United States from Germany three years later. Larry Trimble, a pioneer movie director and animal trainer, was auditioning dogs to star in a movie. In the May 18, 1924, edition of the *New York Times*, he described his first encounter with Etzel at a kennel in White Plains, New York. Larry also told the *Times* how he taught his star, who had been trained as a police dog, to become an actor.

Strongheart's first film was *The Silent Call*, written by Jane Murfin, Larry's wife. It made Strongheart an overnight sensation. Human actors in silent films expressed themselves without speaking; so did Strongheart. Reviewers called him "magnificent" and noted his "intuitive" talent. He was "not one of those tiresome trick dogs." Audiences even thought he cried tears in one scene. As Jane explained in another *New York Times* article, she tailored her scripts to the dog's natural abilities. He was never asked to do anything that wasn't believable.

Only one of his films is still available: *The Return of Boston Blackie*, about an ex-con who tries to go straight with the help of his loyal and clever dog. In it, Strongheart performs some of the stunts that thrilled audiences,

including jumping dozens of feet into the ocean from a revolving amusement park ride.

Strongheart's success in the 1920s prompted legions of dog owners to converge on Hollywood studio lots, hoping to land roles for their pets. One of them was Rin Tin Tin.

Strongheart's uncanny charisma and intuition are celebrated in two books by J. Allen Boone, who cared for the dog for several months while Larry and Jane were traveling. He tells the story of Strongheart's attack on an imposter whom no one else suspected. I borrowed the episode for this book.

Strongheart's star can be found on the Hollywood Walk of Fame along with Rin Tin Tin's and Lassie's. Sadly, Strongheart made only six movies before he died, in 1929, of complications from an injury suffered on the set. His name endures on cans of Strongheart dog food.

BIBLIOGRAPHY

Boone, J. Allen. *Letters to Strongheart*. Harrington Park, NJ: Robert H. Sommer, 1977.
——. *Kinship with All Life*. San Francisco: Harper, 1954.
Orlean, Susan. *Rin Tin Tin: The Life and the Legend*. New York: Simon & Schuster, 2011.

FOR BETSY HESS

Henry Holt and Company, LLC
Publishers since 1866
175 Fifth Avenue
New York, New York 10010
mackids.com

Library of Congress Cataloging-in-Publication Data
McCully, Emily Arnold, author, illustrator.
Strongheart : the world's first movie star dog / Emily Arnold McCully.
pages   cm
Summary: When silent movie director Larry Trimble decides to put Strongheart,
a police dog, into his movies as the lead actor, he must first train him to play with toys and
walk like a regular dog, but Strongheart becomes a sensation until his military training leads
to trouble, and possibly the end of his career. Includes author's note on the real Strongheart.
Includes bibliographical references.
ISBN 978-0-8050-9448-0 (hardback)
[1. Strongheart (Dog)—Fiction. 2. Dogs—Fiction. 3. Trimble, Larry, 1885–1954—Fiction.
4. Murfin, Jane, 1892–1955—Fiction. 5. Silent films—Fiction. 6. Motion pictures—
Production and direction—Fiction.] I. Title.
PZ7.M478415Su 2014   [E]—dc23   2014009189

Henry Holt books may be purchased for business or promotional use. For information
on bulk purchases, please contact Macmillan Corporate and Premium Sales Department
at (800) 221-7945 x5442 or by e-mail at specialmarkets@macmillan.com.

First Edition—2014 / Designed by April Ward
Watercolor and pen and ink on watercolor paper were used to create the illustrations for this book.

Printed in China by Toppan Leefung Printing, Ltd., Dongguan City, Guangdong Province

1 3 5 7 9 10 8 6 4 2

The one pal who
never let them down—
Strongheart!

It was only the
beginning . . .